FOS
3/04

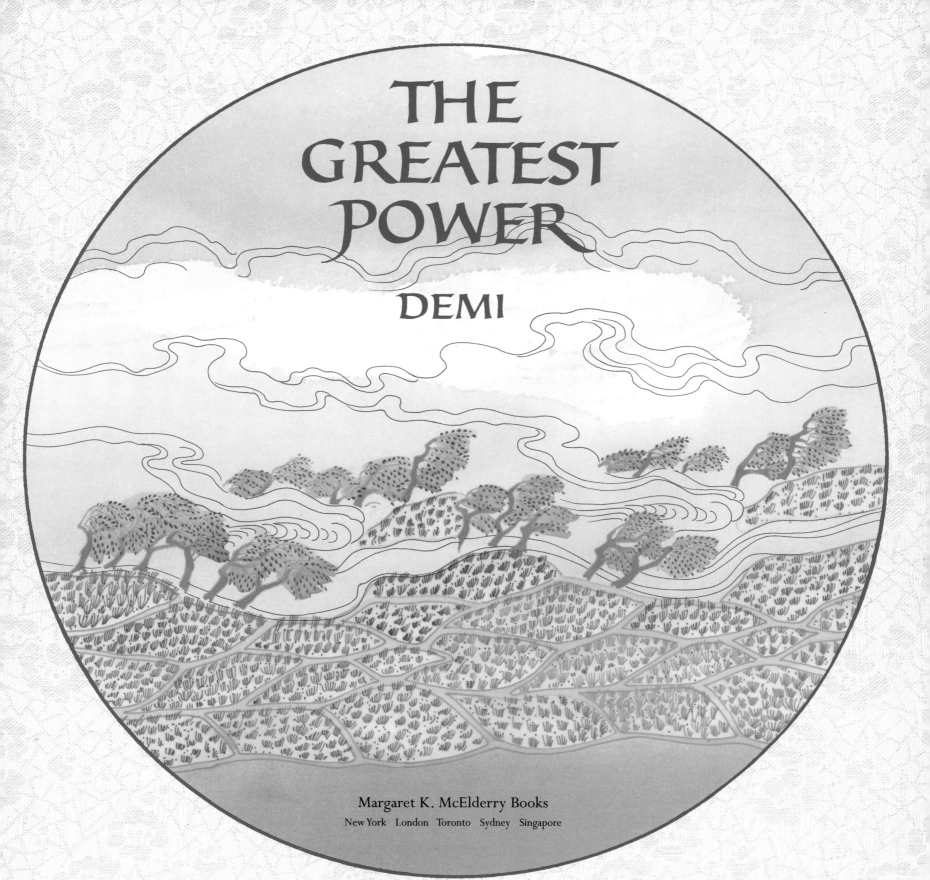

THE GREATEST POWER

DEMI

Margaret K. McElderry Books

New York   London   Toronto   Sydney   Singapore

For all eternity

Margaret K. McElderry Books
An imprint of Simon & Schuster Children's Publishing Division
1230 Avenue of the Americas, New York, New York 10020
Copyright © 2004 by Demi
Book design by Abelardo Martínez
The text for this book is set in Perpetua.
The illustrations for this book are rendered in paint and ink.
Manufactured in China
2 4 6 8 10 9 7 5 3 1
Library of Congress Cataloging-in-Publication Data
Demi.
The greatest power / Demi.— 1st ed.
p. cm.
Summary: Long ago, a Chinese emperor challenges the children of his kingdom to show him
the greatest power in the world, and all are surprised at what is discovered.
ISBN 0-689-84503-0 (hardcover)
[1. Power (Philosophy)—Fiction. 2. China—Fiction.] I. Title.
PZ7.D3925 Gr 2004
[E]—dc21
2002010869

FIRST
EDITION

A long time ago in China there was a boy emperor named Ping who was known throughout the kingdom for his honesty and his love of harmony. The boy emperor enjoyed climbing to the top of the palace and looking through his big telescope at the heavens.

All the millions of stars and the sun and moon and the space in between were in perfect harmony. *My kingdom should be as harmonious as the heavens,* he thought.

Emperor Ping needed the wisest prime minister in all the land to bring the harmony of the heavens to the kingdom. How would the emperor choose such a prime minister? Because he loved the heavens so much, he decided to let the heavens choose.

The next day a proclamation was issued: All the children in the kingdom were to come to the palace. There they would be given a quest that would prove which child was the wisest in the land. That wise child would become the new prime minister.

All the children in the kingdom came from far and wide to learn about Emperor Ping's quest.

"In one year's time," the emperor announced, "we shall have a great parade, and in that parade each of you will show me what you think is the greatest power in the world.

"To know the greatest power in the world
is to know the greatest peace. Whoever knows this harmony
will become the new prime minister."

The emperor concluded, "A wise person
must be able to see the unseen and know the unknown."

The excited children left the palace to begin their quest.

"This is easy," said some of the boys. "Whoever has the greatest weapons has the greatest power in the world. For whoever has the greatest weapons can conquer the world!"

And they began mixing papier-mâché to make axes and shields, spears and swords, bows and arrows, and masks of famous warriors and evil spirits to scare away the enemy.

"This is easy," said some of the girls. "Whoever has the greatest beauty has the greatest power in the world. For whoever has the greatest beauty can command the most powerful commander in the world!"

And they began creating beautiful costumes, each one more intricate and delicate than the next, with colorful silk ribbons, embroidered flowers, sparkling sequins, and golden threads.

printing

paper

paintbrush

kite

umbrella

"This is easy," said some of the more
studious children. "Whoever has
the greatest technology has the
greatest power in the world.
For whoever has the greatest
technology can rule the world!"

compass

water clock

pony express

silk

wheelbarrow

seismograph

porcelain

spaghetti

And they began reconstructing brilliant Chinese ideas that had changed the world. They built clocks and balanced compasses, wove silk and forged iron, crafted porcelain and set movable type, rolled paper and bound books.

bronze and iron

coal

firecrackers

gunpowder

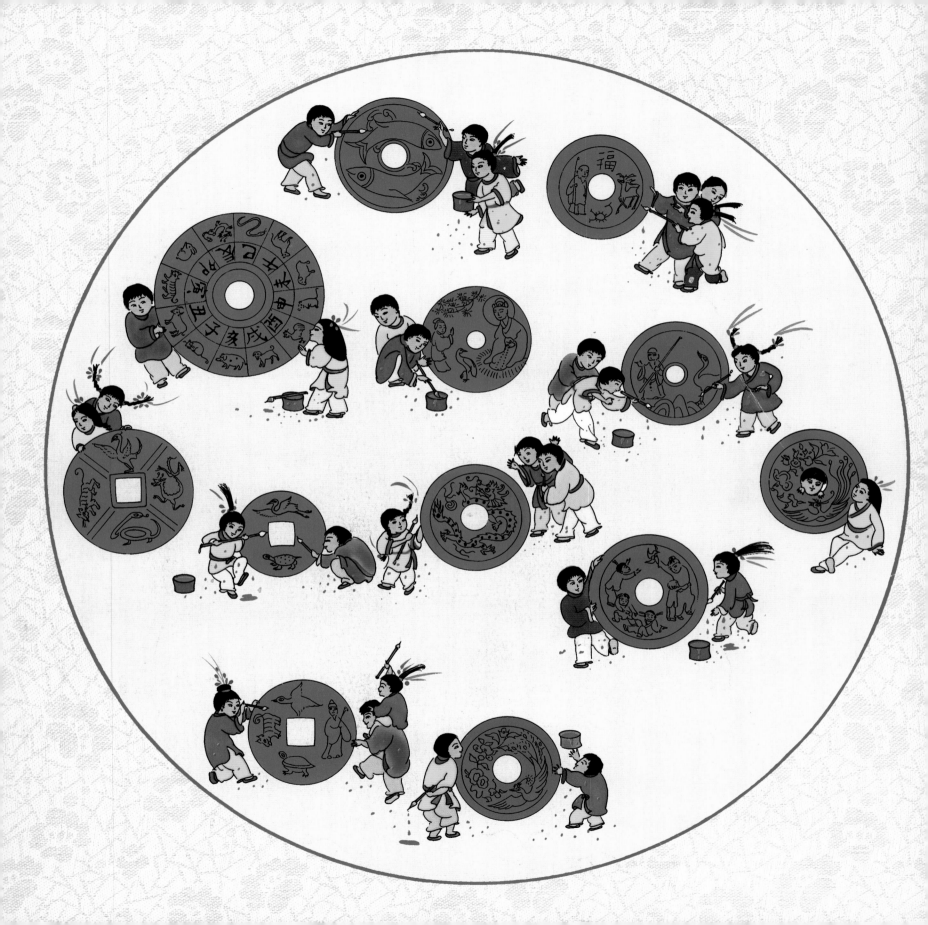

"This is easy," said some of the more practical children. "Whoever has the greatest amount of money has the greatest power in the world.

"For whoever has the greatest amount of money can buy anything in the world!"

And they began making huge golden coins and a statue of the money god, Guan Yu.

Only one child, a little girl
named Sing, remembered the
emperor's words, "A wise person
must be able to see the unseen
and know the unknown."

She sat by a lotus pond and thought
about how armies rise and fall,

how beauty fades,

how money comes and goes,

and how ideas are forever changing.

Could these be the greatest powers
in the world if they didn't even last?

Sing looked at all the beautiful flowers. The lotus was the flower of purity and transformation.

Born from a tiny seed sleeping in the mud, the bud rose through the water on a strong green stem. It rose above the water to bloom into a glorious flower that faced heaven.

What a big story there is in one tiny seed, thought Sing. *How powerful is the force of life!*

By autumn, some boys who thought the emperor possessed the greatest power in the world had made great dragon costumes. The dragon was the emperor's symbol of wealth, wisdom, and power.

By winter, some girls who thought the empress possessed the greatest power behind the throne had made great phoenix costumes. The phoenix was the empress's symbol of loyalty and power.

By spring, Sing still had made nothing to show the emperor. She asked herself, "How can I see the unseen and know the unknown?"

She looked up at the heavens.

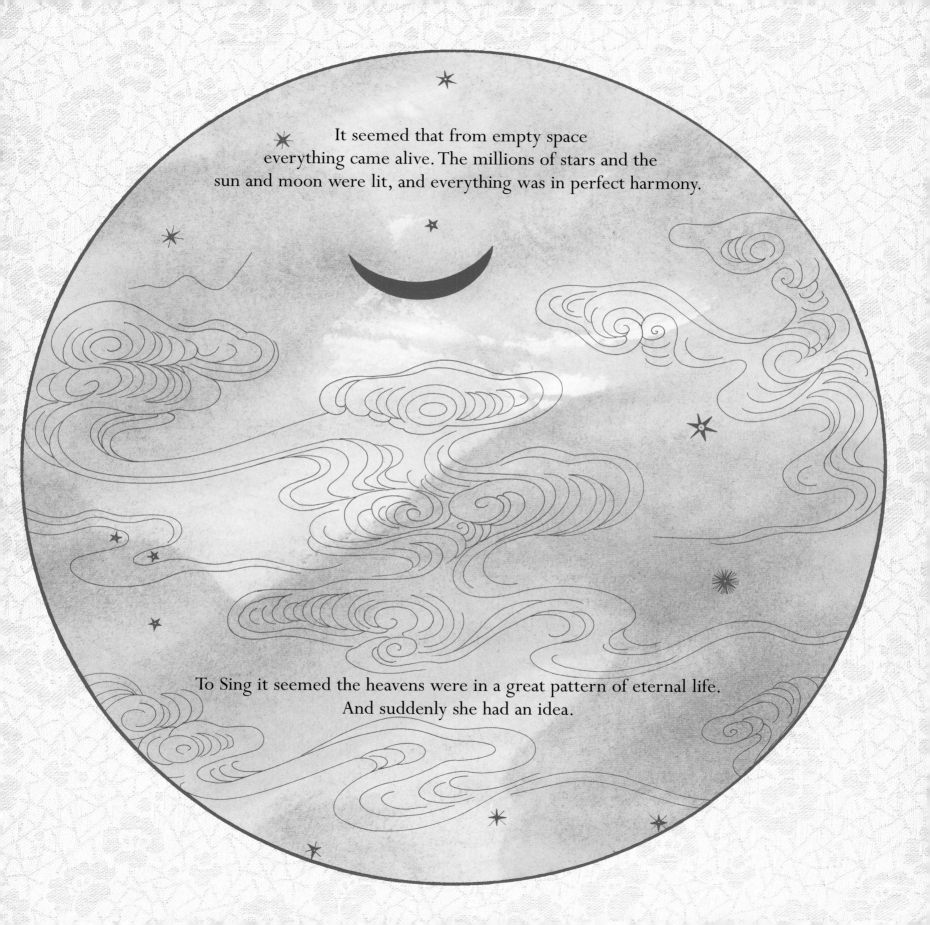

It seemed that from empty space
everything came alive. The millions of stars and the
sun and moon were lit, and everything was in perfect harmony.

To Sing it seemed the heavens were in a great pattern of eternal life.
And suddenly she had an idea.

The great parade day came! All the children of the kingdom came with their most marvelous creations, each one sure that they had figured out the greatest power in the world.

Last of all was Sing, her small hands clenched in front of her.

"Sing!" cried one of the other children. "Don't you have anything to show the emperor?"

"I do have something to show the emperor," Sing said. But the other children just laughed at her.

The children marched before Emperor Ping. With waving flags,
swirling silks, and glistening gold, it was a grand parade.

Emperor Ping did not say a word.

At the end of the parade was Sing.

"Stop the parade!" shouted Emperor Ping. He called Sing to come before him.

"Have you anything to show me? Do you know what the greatest power in the world might be?"

The other children laughed, but Sing held out her hands.

She was holding a lotus seed, which she broke in two before the emperor.

"What is there?" asked Emperor Ping.

"Nothing," said Sing. "And the greatest power in the world."

"How can nothing be the greatest power in the world?" asked the emperor.

"The nothing in this seed is the space in between where life exists," said Sing. "The nothing in this seed is what makes the seed rise from the earth. The nothing in this seed is what is fed by water, air, and the fire of the sun to bloom into a glorious flower that turns its face toward the heavens.

"And when the flower sleeps again, it releases new seeds into the earth, which are fed by water, air, and the fire of the sun to bloom into new flowers. The nothing in this seed is Eternal Life—it continues from seed to seed, forever and ever in perfect harmony. So, Life is the greatest power in the world."

Emperor Ping smiled. He turned to the crowd and declared, "Here is someone who has seen the unseen and knows the unknown. By bringing us this lotus seed, Sing has helped us to see and know the greatest power in the world. She is the wisest child of all the land, and now I name her the new prime minister of all the kingdom."